The Horizon Never Forgets

Poems

Praise for *The Horizon Never Forgets* by Steven T. Moore

Timelines are usually drawn in unwavering straight lines—point A to point B, across the human seas of birth and life and death. But what artists do is create little circles along the way. Call them twisters, water spouts. Call them the chaos of life's struggle in an unbalanced world. We poets, especially, sit on the back of the ship and sum up the storms humanity just sailed through, giving voice to all those feelings swirled up inside.

In this poetry collection, Steven T. Moore leads us down into this painful labyrinth, this deep circle of despair, to the heartbreaking things one human can do to another. But yet, just when all hope seems lost, Moore returns, poem after poem, to the image of his mother—that eternal vision of unconditional love.

This is not a political work. It is a humanitarian work that only a poet of Moore's caliber could do—a coming of age in America's timeline that leads up to a parent having to say goodbye to her child, having to leave a world she so desperately wished to make better for the next generation. This is the universal desire to open the heart—that boundless, colorless, greater good that beats within us all, as Moore so eloquently writes in the last poem of the book, "Goodnight": "Now in this cold hospital room, / I look into her hailstormed eyes / and I think I know what she wants / as she points to a bookcase not there. / I recite poetry by Langston Hughes, / Jericho Brown, Maya Angelou / softly into her ear. She smiles, I weep. / She trembles, reaches over to wipe / away a few of my tears. / Stars rush into the room."

—karla k. Morton, 2010 Texas State Poet Laureate
and author of *Turbulents & Fluids*

What does it mean to pull back the mask "that grins and lies"? To remove it completely, to bare the blackness of one's grief, one's rage, one's pain on the page? To make your reader face it, feel it? To tell the stories of trauma on the margins of integration? To give voice to generational suffering? To have these stories resonate within the context of classic lines by Langston Hughes and Paul Laurence Dunbar? In *The Horizon Never Forgets*, Steven Moore drops us into the kaleidoscope trauma, the multifaceted fear of racist violence, the anxiety of caregiving for his aging parents, the devastating repeating cycle of loss and grief on the personal and national levels as one Black person after another succumbs to racist violence. This unflinching collection of poems reveals the complexity of Black male rage, giving us insight into debilitating horrors of negotiating medical, educational, cultural, interpersonal, and structural racism. They say that we must feel our trauma to heal it. Perhaps this powerful collection of narrative poems opens up space for the possibility of transcendence for all who empathize with the struggle.

—Cherise A. Pollard, author of *Outsiders*

The Russian poet Anna Akhmatova said, "You wish you could put back together what has been torn apart, but there is no such glue." The pages of *The Horizon Never Forgets* are torn-apart pages, pages torn apart by love, hate, racism, and honesty. Steven T. Moore confronts us with a combination of hard realism and lyrical forgiveness. Into this poet's world we are taken, and the only way out is to listen.

—Earl S. Braggs, author of *Moving to Neptune: New & Selected*

Steven Moore's vision is clear, even as time and family and justice slip underneath him. In *The Horizon Never Forgets*, Moore writes for his mother and her "lifetime of fighting / for her sons to be free." He writes for "her hailstormed eyes." He writes her "a bookcase not there." Moore's poems search simultaneously for the "way out" of injustice and the way in. Here he is able to stay with pain—personal and systemic—and so allows his readers to do the same.

—Leah Naomi Green, author of *The More Extravagant Feast* and winner of the 2019 Walt Whitman Award

At first glance, Steven Moore's debut poetry collection, *The Horizon Never Forgets*, feels too hot to hold. The rage. The racism. The needless losses experienced daily by Black Americans in our society. But when you open your mind and heart to the indignities and injustices revealed in these pages, you see, really see, how looking the other way only further scars and berates our fellow humans simply going about their lives. Moore's rage is bookended by childhood, where he learned to smile and nod in the face of bullying and caricature, to learning to live without his mother's love and support. Still, Moore is lifted, despite the growing list of unarmed Blacks murdered by police and others, by the redemptive power of poetry, the remembered lines of Langston Hughes his mother recited to him as a boy. Let us not look away from the horizon ablaze with prejudice and fear. Let us name the names lost and not forget that we are all connected. Let us not stop hoping and working for change.

—Linda Parsons, author of *Valediction: Poems and Prose*

The Horizon Never Forgets

Poems

Steven T. Moore

MADVILLE
PUBLISHING

LAKE DALLAS, TEXAS

FIRST EDITION

Requests for permission to reprint or reuse material
from this work should be sent to:

Permissions
Madville Publishing
PO Box 358
Lake Dallas, TX 75065

Author Photo: Matt Maxwell
Cover Art: *End of the World* by Emily Rankin
Cover Design: Kimberly Davis

ISBN: 978-1-963695-15-1 paperback
978-1-963695-16-8 ebook
Library of Congress Control Number: 2024944368

To my loving mother, Clara L. Moore

*To all the Black people who are
having a difficult time breathing*

Contents

II. The horizon never forgets

III. The moon follows me and my grief

What is it you wanted me to reconcile myself to? I was born here, almost 60 years ago. I'm not going to live another 60 years. You always told me, "It takes time." It's taken my father's time, my mother's time, my uncle's time, my brothers' and my sisters' time. How much time do you want for your progress?

—James Baldwin

Who Am I?

I apply for a job. The prospective employer throws the traditional questionnaire at me. I take out a pen to muddle through standard questions. The first section asks me for full name, date of birth, social security number. I come to the familiar question about my race. Last year I checked "Black," but this year I have to select another label.

___Caucasian
___African American
___Asian American
___European American
___Hispanic American
___Native American
___Other

Who am I? What am I this time? At one time in this land of freedom and opportunity, my enduring race would check "Colored." Then after many years, our status transformed into the term "Negro." Then "Negro" was changed to "Black" because "Negro" reminded us of slavery. The forms again changed from "Black" to "African" because of the belief that all American Blacks originated from Africa. Then it switched to "Afro-American" which was soon changed to "African American." Today, there are still those who do not know what to call us. Some say I am "Black," and others say "African American." So, who am I this time?

During the days when I was younger and innocent, I often asked myself what I was going to be when I grew up and wondered who I was inside the child known as Steven Moore. I found out who I was after attending grade school in Montgomery, Alabama, where my brother and I were the only Black kids in the class and somehow we ended up in the back row. I remember our teacher thought it was amusing to read us the illustrated tale *Little Black Sambo*. The class laughed and snickered at the drawings of this little African boy with kinky wild hair, huge bulging eyes, and large red lips. After school, kids taunted me with many names: blackie, burnt coal, grease monkey, chocolate

Easter bunny, burnt match, dirty Q-tip, brillo pad, darkie, colored—the list goes on and on. Am I really any of these?

As I ran home, the cruel names and the drawings of *Little Black Sambo* raced through my mind. I gazed into the mirror, examining my hair, my eyes, my lips. The little Black boy in the mirror stared back at me, and I saw the kinky hair, the bulging eyes, the watermelon slices. I wanted to rub off the black smudge that was my skin, but it refused to comply. Inside the sanctuary of my bedroom, I looked myself up in *Webster's Dictionary*:

BLACK (blak) adj.
1. opposite to white; the color of coal
2. having dark, colored skin and hair
3. Negro
4. dark and dirty
5. without light
6. evil and wicked
7. sad and dismal

I threw the book on the floor in a rage and just sat there at my desk, my black face staring out the window, searching for someone, searching for something to answer my question: "Who am I?"

In junior high, the history teacher asked, "Okay, class … what do you know about the history of Blacks?" One kid said, "Black kids are kids who rap and make funny noises, jump up and down with those Malcolm X hats." He thought he was being funny, and so did the teacher, who said nothing while an amused smile appeared on his face. In a neutral voice, he took out a book and read to us about "Blacks." Some students laughed as he fumbled around trying to relay African American history, a topic he knew nothing about.

Later still in high school, I watched African Americans act in TV sitcoms, such as *Sanford and Son, Good Times, The Jeffersons,* and *What's Happening!* Hollywood tried desperately to show "the realities of the Black experience"—but failed. They created characters like Fred Sanford and J. J. Walker for fun and a good laugh. I saw believable white actors like Ed Asner and Mary Tyler Moore who portrayed successful, proud Americans, but I guess Blacks were simply a "happy-go-lucky" people, whose role was to make people laugh with their silly antics.

In college, I was asked stupid questions: "Do you use grease in your hair?" "Can you dance?" "Is it true? Do Blacks really love fried chicken and watermelon?" "Why do so many Black people talk and dress just like white people?" "Can you play basketball?" "I know you can play football, basketball, and you can dance because all Blacks are good athletes and entertainers, right? Plus, you have natural rhythm!" Every time I heard these questions, I burst out with nervous laughter, for through the years, I have learned how to laugh at racism. I have learned how to sigh at what people say about my race. Some people just do not know us, but my question is: Does anyone know us?

Who am I?

I.

Shimmering

        sunlight

                and

                        dark

                                rain

Fifth Grade Swim Trip on a Partly Cloudy Day and Beautiful Brown Feet

The yellow sun
staring down at us
as we play,
sing, jeer, and laugh.

Crystal, clean water
splashes our feet
as we run along
the edges of the pool.
White feet all around me—
glimmering in sunlight.
Kids stare down at my feet
as if something is wrong,
something seems to be wrong with me.

Later in art class, I grab brown paint—
some splatters all over the white, clean canvas.
Look at what you've done, the teacher says,
Look at what you've done.
I continue painting,
begin creating two brown feet.
Sun finally breaks through the shade.
My feet now look like tree trunks
burrowing into the earth,
moving beyond the canvas,
bursting with life.

Arrival

A steely, cold Monday morning
wind brushes up and down my naked neck,

eventually slaps my head,
refusing to be ignored on this day

where black birds down my street
hang their heads, refusing to sing

as the sun wrestles with gray streaming
clouds. Each step on frozen ground,

sounds of crackling fire, and my mind
strolls down long hallways, recalling

summer afternoons, lazy white and purple
flowers nestled among the prairie, daylight

inviting heads of trees to nod in balmy
winds like my mother's embrace

welcoming me after a long journey.

After We Read "Theme for English B"

My white students ask,

What's it like being you?

I wonder if it's that simple to answer.

I'm middle-aged, Black, born in Virginia
where young and old white men, unmasked,
torches in hand, held a march
a few years ago near cloud-concrete
sidewalks where I walked
to school down Carpenter Lane.

My brother and I are the only splashes
of living color in a class brimming with white faces,
teeth sparkling bright as day, their mouths
filled at breakfast with milk and Captain Crunch
now spewing out *Nigger* and *Blackie* at us.
I want to vomit but can't.

Transferred to another school with bricks
laid down by freed slaves,
I learn new words in English class.
I can't seem to find the right ones to express
what I am seeing and feeling.

Black boy hangs from a tree.
Blood stains grass below.
Cops, firemen, neighbors stand around.
Even birds are quiet this Wednesday morning.

I remember my friend, my neighbor killed himself.
Tired of being Black, being invisible, being nothing.
I quickly learned math that day as I subtracted another Black life
and calculated the cost of racism.

I remember when Mother saw our teacher,
who faithfully attended the church
with red doors a few blocks away
from the school, hitting me and my twin
because she hated blackness.

I remember the principal slammed his door
in my mother's face
as she yelled and complained.

I remember cops pulling me over,
searching my car for drugs,
their grimy hands migrating
all over my black body.
Found nothing.
Thought I was a thug driving a stolen car.

After I finish this class, it will be time
to take a walk to clear my head.
Try to calm down, try to breathe.
Don't want to alarm any whites in this neighborhood,
so I turn down Kendrick Lamar
and start humming Mozart.

Don't want to die today—

At this moment, though, I wonder
as my white students turn away,
surprised, stunned,
or perhaps simply amused,
if any of them
would ever want to be me,
even a small part of me?

I have no answers as the door closes
and I'm left with white chalk and white paper.

I read the poem again.
I think of Langston Hughes
alone in his room at the Harlem Y.
This is my theme for English B.

Singing Train

The train, a sharp soprano
serenading me miles away
from downtown finally stops,
a wind hitting a wall,
nowhere to go, legs resting
before departing again.
I embrace my brother
after years of separation,
his clothes barely hanging
on, lingering leaves
left behind after the storm.

Our grandparents, our mother
have gone, departed
to another land in the beyond,
we feel them
as we hold each other in our arms,
not wanting to let go.

On trains as a boy,
I saw the blooming light
window to window, flickering,
felt the warm ghost of summer
hovering over my skin.

Squeezing my brother
now in this moment, tightly
holding onto memories:
cities built on beaches.
Fireflies bursting across
dark orange skies.
The golden sun begins
to close its eyes,
the singing train will soon
fade into night.

Dropping Down into the River

for Jack Pine

My 80-year-old
wheelchaired neighbor
from the yellow house
is a struggling sailor rowing
down our black paved street,
windy day with only a few joggers,
a little girl chalking her driveway,
a red truck coughing as I walk outside.

I blink, become that boy again
playing in sand, creating little bodies
for my imaginary town.

They are beautiful,
don't last forever,
rain carries them away.

I look up, notice my neighbor
sculling a parcel of mail
blown down the street.
I help, present it to him.
He gets up from his wheelchair,
embraces me as orange
and red leaves swirl around us.
Miles away, we look like twisted
string lights, embers from chimneys,
stars dressed in red
on crisp fall days.

We are caught up together
by the wind,
and in this moment,
I'm ready to drop
down into the river with him.

Still a Slave

I feel the whips
whenever I'm stopped
by cops, my black body
out of place in this tiny neighborhood
as white families simply drive by
pointing
       gawking
              at me
on their way to where white families go.

I drag chains at work,
their clanking unheard by the educated people
with professional smiles who turn
the other way when racism stands
beside my desk and begs a ride home with me.
I walk into the cotton fields of the ICU
where my black diabetic mother
is hooked up to a ventilator,
pumping air into her black broken body,
a lifetime of fighting
for her sons to be free
and my elderly father
holds her hand
all night long,

he who fought in wars where fellow soldiers
hated him for being a dark moon in their skies,
his soulful eyes that would not shy away
from truth, and now he must explain
to worried white faces inside
the so-called post-racial elevator
that he is not there to rob or hurt them
but just to be with his wife.

All night long I listen to ambulances,
doctors, nurses rushing to receive
the black bodies piling up,
sponging more black blood down the drain,
and I wish they'd stop telling me
we've got this,
everything is going to be okay.

Still Here

A drab blue shirt hangs
on a lean clothesline
down the street,
flapping long arms
into the cool, fall wind.
It is the only one
hanging there,
as if left
by mistake,
forgotten, ignored,
unloved. I remember
a blond boy with dirty
nails lying about me,
informing Mrs. Penn
I shoved him in line.
She made me stand
in the corner next
to the coat rack
and old pile of books,
undisturbed,
unresponsive. Hours
stack, still standing.
Lunch time, she forgot
about me, eating
last night's pasta
at her desk.
Then she peered up,
eyes wide,
horrified. Then and now
I'm a ghost,
yet I'm still here.
I'm still here.

They Carried Me Home Over Their Shoulders

A yellow house
on the corner, white trim,
wide open windows, red door,
an elderly woman wearing
a sunflower apron emerges,
waves at me. The wind hums,
branches sway. Golden pheasants
from afternoon dreams lead me
into the woods.
I imitate the tall trees,
run away, follow the sun.
The wind tastes like home.
A calm river flows inside me.
I hear my grandmother's voice,
lift my hands, wave at the silver clouds.
They surprise me, swoop down,
pick me up. They carry me
home over their shoulders.

Monday Rain

I am with my brother
cheering in soaked streets
on Carpenter and Y, where
trees and houses are melting
from a distance. Our raincoats,
the color of bees
churning honey, our red boots
shine brighter than a screaming
firetruck. We stretch our arms,
praying for the sky and sun to lift us up.
We are so alive, completely free,
we don't need umbrellas,
we're not afraid of getting wet
this afternoon. We sing above
the noise of the city, can't even
hear the train, a French horn
screeching into the wind.
We are loud enough for windows
to shake and thunder to applaud.
We embrace each other
not wanting this rain nor this moment
to fall and slip away.

A Hundred Mondays

Hasn't rained for months,
the grass outside, brittle and brown,
crunches with each step, tiny
echoes of death, a hollow
desert around me.
The kitchen sink, a landfill of dishes,
my bed, unmade for weeks,
TV is on, sparks of the living,
I ignore them all. Their jokes, unfunny
and unreal. I have been here before.

Waiting tables at Denny's, running back
and forth, fulfilling every wish:
bring me more coffee,
hurry up with those eggs, bring me the check.
I slam their dirty dishes into the bins,
remembering David, red shirt, thick
white stripe across his chest, kids
shoving and yelling *black ape* at him.
Did it daily. Neighborhood
infested with drugs, alcohol, and blood.
He died two nights ago. Suicide. I see
his silent face, black spiraling hair,
arms at rest inside the coffin.

Every Monday, every day seems the same.
Waiting for that pungent, musty odor,
weighing down the air,
that intoxicating smell of fresh wood.
Waiting for that rain to come.

Stuttering

I.

is hard to control when you're a nervous
young boy
stumbling over words in the dark
hitting furniture
knocking down lamps
or during daylight
striking out on the baseball field
with a chorus of round-faced kids
laughing out of key.

II.

When I taught my first English class
that little stuttering schoolboy
returned to haunt me,
remind me
that he was still nervous, still afraid
of ghosts and goblins
walking the beat on our Halloween streets.

III.

My mother shakes
whenever she is nervous.

IV.

In line at J.C. Penney's
two cops in blue
stand behind her

their golden badges
shining like the face
of a mad train birthed screaming out of a tunnel.

V.

Far from the cash register
I notice what is going on
quietly walk up
see
the woman I love and trust
shaking
not saying a word.

I begin stuttering and screaming
inside my head.

VI.

Tonight I count
the empty chairs of my classroom.

I remember
my mother and begin to calm down.
It's as if we're counting together
praying together
for all the guns
to remain silent.

Grins and Lies

We wear the mask that grins and lies,
It hides our cheeks and shades our eyes.
—Paul Laurence Dunbar

The poet was right.
We wear the mask

each day still we rise.
A Black man like me

cannot reveal what I'm feeling
as I stand in front of a white class

speak of Blacks in chains
crawling with the bright

sun behind them, their sweat,
their blood, falling hail.

Coughing dust, picking cotton,
black crows flying above.

I sit in meetings, never raise
my voice, calmly smile and nod.
Think about black bodies
being assaulted and killed

while crunching numbers
on spreadsheets in front of me.

Most nights I have
the same dream:

I'm the scarecrow
stuck in the field,

cannot move nor speak.
I wake up, put on my mask

that grins and lies.
Let them think otherwise.

Rainbow

Feet of a young teenager
shuffle inside the oldest bookstore
in Southlake, Texas, his fluffy
blonde hair bobbling with each step,
a few colorful stripes are exposed
as he walks toward me, a faint rainbow
crying across the horizon.
Legs barely breathe inside
tight skinny jeans as he
finally stands beside me.
He takes a book off the shelf,
Selected Poems by Pablo Neruda.
His fingers gingerly play
through the white pages
like new keys on a grand piano.
He makes eye contact with me.
His fingers tighten, struggles to say
hello. I want to tell him
everything is going
to be okay, hang in there.
Instead I say *hi* and he walks
away. I imagine him as a kite
struggling to fly in the wind
on a partly sunny day,
birds on each side,
ushering him to the clouds.

October Morning

I stagger into the kitchen,
grab coffee, waiting for toast
and eggs. Out my window a brown
and white wren stretches,
leans forward, opens mouth,
delivers first notes of a new song,
an invitation for dawn to crawl
out of bed. A dog barks
a few doors down,
stirring my mind to recall
a dream from last night:

I'm lost, scared,
running, trembling,
my feet heavy.
Above me silky yellow
skies appear, kissing blue
waters, red leaves end
their rustling to watch.
Sinking into grasslands
I hear a distant voice
calling me home.

Now on this quiet October
morning, I find myself
staring down
at a shiny knife
as I butter
a warm piece of toast.

Grandfather Clock

I purchase it
from the downtown antique store
at 833 Butternut
where relics wave from windows
begging for someone to catch a glimpse,
pick them up, and carry them home.
I set it in the corner of my living room
where it becomes my grandfather
quietly standing.
sometimes I forget he's there
until I hear him during odd times
throughout the day chiming,
murmuring underneath his breath
about the hell he experienced:
dirty white boys laugh
calling him *Nigger* and *monkey*
at the town square,
white girls in yellow dresses
play hopscotch
throwing rocks at his feet,
seeing how high he could jump,
tick tock, tick tock.
my grandfather picked cotton for Mister Edwards
who made promises he never kept,
he always begged my grandfather to sing
swing low, sweet chariot on Sunday afternoons,
tick tock, tick tock.
there were times I caught him
crying at night and wondered
if he hated his life,
a Black man who went unnoticed,
hiding in corners,
hands in pockets,
tick tock, tick tock.
wish I could see him now,

his gray black wavy hair
ocean waves at midnight.
his skin was softest hay
at playtime during summer.
his brown eyes
lonely clouds behind the sun.
tick tock, tick tock, tick tock.

Here in the Country

A yellow button-down
shirt hangs undisturbed
in a closet behind
our winter coats,
belonged to my
grandfather,
tall, slender man,
thin tree standing
alone some nights
along the woods. I loved
leaning against him,
the smell of smoked
leaves and cinnamon
from his pipe, always
on Sundays. His black
suede hat stared
often into a dark sky
that had no answers.
He became farmless
when white men stole
everything from him,
my mother tried
to explain when I was too
young to understand.

I now know why
she becomes solemn
here in the country,
why she hates
roaming cattle
and crickets singing
during the arrival
of the red sky
and the bitter
moon and stars.

This Country Does Not Love Us Back

for Doc Rivers

you would rather us
shut up, dribble,
bounce basketballs,
throw them into white nets
that with every swoosh remind
us of what we heard
when slave ships rocked
up and down on cold waters.

you would rather see us run
back and forth
sweat pounding on
floors like the tears slaves
shed while their naked
backs were whipped for
your pleasure.

you would rather have us play hard
until we drop like the fierce sun
after a long day
only for your kids to hang us
as posters in their bedrooms.

you'll sleep tight as nightmares bounce
inside my head, Blacks
hanging, swaying back and forth
like silent basketball nets
when the lights are off.

you'll cut nets down for our Black
brothers and sisters murdered
while we watch and listen to you cheer
shaking pom-poms, blowing air horns
from the stands.

Dead Flowers

On a spring Saturday morning
my mother buys
sunflowers
to brighten our house
on 4th and Pine.

My mother comes inside
tells me about
the white cashier
staring at her
following her
around the shop
sizing her up
like she does
early each day
as the red roses
arrive ready to be
chopped and
forced to fit inside
glass vases.

Rushing out of the shop
my mother finally
hears the white cashier
mumbling
stupid Nigger
from the same mouth
that must have
kissed her children
after packing their lunches
and wishing them a good day
as they left for school.

The next day
on my way

to work
I noticed the
sunflowers upside

down
in our trash can
with a few
petals
being carried away
by local ants
hungry on this quiet
spring morning.

Early Morning Voices

I can't sleep. Walk outside,
porchlight still on, black sky
speaking to the Earth below.
Cannot understand the language.
The calm morning air, taste of the void,
rests on my tongue. I accept it.
Night creatures whisper
and whirl in bushes. They're restless.
Look up, waiting for the sun to speak.
It is the first day of fall semester
and I'm getting ready to go to my office.
I remember long ago, Mother
reciting a Langston Hughes poem
as she walked me to school: *I've known rivers:*
Ancient, dusky rivers. My soul has grown
deep like the rivers. Moments later,
I see a young couple walking their dog,
a city bus sailing along, a pale blue sky
looking down without comment.

Eclipse

Looks like night beginning
to fall again. It is only noon.
Sun shimmers on red and yellow
leaves outside, tiny fires bursting
with delight, swaying in the gentle wind,
while I hear the music of Chopin
join them in my head. Sidewalks
all around, pristine and untouched,
a scene from my youth.
I'm five, my father
sings a song. I can't remember
the tune now. He swings
me around in circles. I'm flying, sunlight
glowing all over my body.
I am new, I am free.
The world suddenly fades.
For a few minutes
everything turns dark.

Pumping Gas on a Sunny Day, US Highway 80 E in Abilene, TX

I'm trying to drive
and obey
black & white
signs

my mind races
to the nearest gas station
before everything
zeros out on me

I'm empty today
because of Charlottesville
a city in Virginia
the state of my birth

a place where white
unmasked
supremacists
unleashed raging fists
where birds have ended their singing

I pull into a gas station
grab the nozzle
fumes choking me

a black pickup truck
decorated with rebel flags
occupies the spot in front of me

out steps
a large white man
wearing jeans
stained white t-shirt
leather cowboy boots pressing

down on the hot
black pavement below

this man leans his eyes into me
and I wonder
what he is thinking

or if he is like one of them
who earnestly prays for me to hang
from a tree

fear turns to rage
rage turns to disgust
all at the same time

I start smelling the gas
see the torches in their hands

then the fire
until I hear the pump click off
and he finally drives away

A Poem for All the White People Who Just Don't Get It

I want to slap your stupid white face
      very hard, make it bright red like
    tomatoes in full bloom out back next to the shed.

I want your white son to be falsely arrested then
    strip-searched while I down another
        cheeseburger from McDonald's.

I want your white 78-year-old grandmother to cry
       hard April rain where floods rush in to carry me
    downhill with a cool breeze that makes me smile.

I want your white daughter to feel the stings
    of honey bees
    and black cops tasing her in new skinny-fit pants
    purchased from Lululemon.

I want to hear white people complain
    about being mistreated then
    I will say these words while sipping on
    southern iced tea, "It is what it is!"

Me Like Black

I'm a brown
wheat field
ready for the harvest.

Black young boy in blue
who stares into a sky
of sailboats and clouds.

Crows dressed
like midnight
peck away at my dreams.

Sunny day, bright clouds above.
Kid yells Nigger.
It begins to rain.

White kids
pelt snowballs
at my black face.

Class snickers
during reading
of *Little Black Sambo.*

Got learner's permit today.
Freedom to drive.
Mom begins to worry.

Downtown train
hums and sings
as I doze off at nightfall.

Howling wind and rain
beat down my front door
begging to come inside.

Elderly woman
aproned in sunflowers
hides drained eyes from me.

Black body sways
beneath a piece of sturdy rope.
Mississippi flies buzz around.

Police pull me over
weapons drawn.
I grip the wheel.

Old woman tightly
holds her purse
on elevator ride with me.

Students nod
as I teach Langston Hughes.
I put down the white chalk.

Mom in hospital
bed struggles
to wave goodbye.

The cold feel
of my mother's coffin.
I nearly stop breathing.

Watching the morning news
another Black guy shot dead.
I throw toast and eggs into the sink.

I'm a dead dried
field stretching out
in the scorching sun.

II.

The

        horizon

                never

                        forgets

Skittles

for Trayvon Martin, 13th Anniversary of his death

I love Skittles
I eat them all the time
those colorful bite-sized tiny bullets
thrust me into a universe
of pure happiness and delight.

Taste the rainbow.

I become that kid again
transformed into an astronaut
on a daring mission to save
my family and friends
from an impending asteroid
poised to wipe them out.

Taste the rainbow.

Or after a handful of skittles
I become Superman with an invincible red cape
flying into a burning building without fear
and rescuing two kids
screeching at the door of death.

Taste the rainbow.

But now, I hate skittles.

Trayvon who looked like me at age 17
had a craving for candy that evening.

Wish I could have been there
Wish I could have been
that astronaut to send him to the moon

or to a planet where race doesn't matter at all.
Wish I could have been Superman,
flying down with my cape to protect him
from that one bullet.

Taste the rainbow.

Wish I could have stopped
those purple, yellow, green, red, orange raindrops
from falling to the ground that night.

Because of Trayvon,
the rainbow has a different taste.

Bulletproof Castles

for George Floyd

I'm reading a children's book
about knights and castles to Mrs. Walker's class,
their tiny faces beaming as I read each page.
But this morning, I'm only watching
the Black boys and Black girls
because of last night's news:
another unarmed Black person dead.

I turn the page, see the Black boy in blue.
He will be delayed during 3:30 pickup today
because his father's body
was unable to withstand the pressure
of cops bearing down on his head.

I turn the page, see the Black girl in yellow
with crumbs of homemade biscuits
jailed inside her braided hair, the one who will miss
her grandmother's breakfasts,
that kind old woman who lived in Florida for years
before being gunned down on 7th and Hickory,
an accidental shooting they say.
The breakfast dishes still rest in the sink.

I turn the page, see the fidgety Black boy wearing red.
His mother, who works at Walmart down the street,
will be dead tonight from walking out her backdoor.
Heard a commotion while ironing clothes,
no idea about the 911 call.
They sprayed her down with bullets along with her daisies
blooming by the windowsill.
Mistake they said. The iron is still on in the kitchen.

45

I finish the book,
praying that bullets and blood
will not change the color of their sun and clouds
drawn hours ago now tucked away inside backpacks
purchased last week during the back-to-school sale.

I leave the room, wishing for knights
to carry these Black boys and Black girls home,
lock them behind doors,
tuck them safely inside bulletproof castles.

It Feels Like Blood

I walk into the local supermarket,
6th and Elm. Hopeful.
This sunny afternoon,
only a few clouds out.
Inside, the floors shine,
white clouds cut into blocks
beneath my feet. The lights above,
tiny artificial moons, everything
glistens because of them: green apples,
yellow bananas, freshly cut
red meats at the butcher's counter.
On the floor, I find a newspaper
that belongs upfront at the news rack.
It tells the story of a young Black man:
Jayland Walker, 25, most sincere, most
kindhearted person, he was a brother
to me, friends say. Was a wrestler, too.
He's one of the sweetest, his coach said.
I see his picture, his bright smile, his black
wavy hair, his brown eyes,
I see the dark autumn night
when 46 police bullets tore him.
Had no gun. His face. His cracked body.
Can't shake it.
Drop the carton of eggs in my hands,
bend down, white, broken shells
everywhere. The yellow, thick
yolk. Sticky. All over my fingers.
It feels like blood.
My racing heart
searches for a way
out. I am sweating,
my face, hot. I know how
clouds that cannot rain feel.
I know how they feel on days like this.

Another Unarmed Black Man,
Earl Moore, 35, Dies in Police Custody

I hear the moaning of the downtown
train: loud, somber, always
stirs me deep within. Seems out of place.
Wonder what my neighbors think and feel
whenever they hear it each day. Maybe it doesn't
bother them. Making pancakes today,
whisking eggs, milk, butter,
vanilla extract inside the glass bowl.
Looks like sunlight, honey from bees.
Mother thought otherwise when she was ill.
It looks like thick blood,
looks like blood, she would say. I can't
concentrate on the task at hand. Still thinking
about her words. The pancakes this morning:
brown, uneven, flat.
I take a bite.
Throw the dishes into the sink.

Black Monday

I pound my fist
upon the chalkboard
hoping
to wake
student
sleeping
second
to last row
on this Monday morning
after fall break.

I pound
while
dissecting
"Theme for English B"
by Langston Hughes
in front of a white class
as white chalk
snows
all over my black skin.

I'm trying to concentrate
trying to keep pace
with this frigid, 8 a.m. class
trying hard not
to think about the frigid news
from this morning
another
black
body
falls

this time
it's a Black Dallas-Fort Worth woman
Atatiana Jefferson

in her own home
in her bedroom
in front of her 8-year-old nephew
shot dead by a white cop

"You are white… perhaps
you don't want to be a part of me,"
writes Langston Hughes.

While reading these lines
I look up
see no movement
no changes
in cold faces
of those listening
and the rage within
simmers
as I pound on the board

replicating
sounds of bullets
entering her black body
pound
pound
pound that board
eyes
become red
sweat
begins
body quakes

and the
black eraser,
the black coffin

quietly
falls
to the floor

and
that student
finally
wakes up.

Stale Summer Wind

I keep having the same
dream, bare cupboards,
empty cotton fields,
red roses nowhere in sight.
The wind is warm, it is summer.
Wake up, walk around wooden
crackling floors of my house,
sounds like fire, naked
thoughts haunting me
with each step:
Black slaves
working white fields,
sun melts their backs,
must keep going
or death will come,
keep humming,
keep singing.
Today, sun peeks
its head through
the branches, it stares
at me as I prune the roses
near my front porch.
The wind brushes my neck.
It is friendly, it is soothing,
I keep going. I remember
the morning news: Ralph Yarl,
16-year-old Black boy,
honors student,
plays the bass clarinet,
went to the wrong house,
shot twice, once in the head,
the other in the arm
while picking up
his twin brothers.
I am thinking of him,

Breonna Taylor,
Ahmaud Arbery,
Botham Jean,
Tamir Rice,
Earl Moore,
Tyre Nichols,
Daunte Wright,
Atatiana Jefferson.
I start
humming and singing,
hear a passerby say
he must be happy,
must be really happy today.

Jogging with Ahmaud Arbery

I'm moving down Freedom Lane
black naked feet
protected inside
white Nike Air
I keep trying to fly yet can't
as each foot rises and falls

pounding the pavement below
on this cool evening with the naughty
wind tickling my legs and neck
a few pigeons cooing
moon jumping in the sky
refusing to be ignored.

I think I see Wanted signs
hanging on every lamppost
on both sides of the street.
Each one bears a black face and a name
the ones with red banners
using bright yellow letters
to announce DEAD.

My breathing quickens as I run past
faces of boys and girls
with warm summer afternoon smiles
and playground eyes fresh as linen
then the posters for mothers and fathers
aunts and uncles with hands soft
as Arkansas cotton.

Dozens more assault my view
as I keep running
trucks roaring up behind
stench of tobacco and cartridge smoke

chase down to the ground
the last breath
of my prayer to fly.

Ahmaud Arbery:
Trial Verdict Just Announced

Black people know the taste of smoke and blood,
that lingering tang, polluted fumes, thick oil
and mud mingled together, coursing inside
our mouths whenever verdicts come down.
Today I'm unemotional, unsure how to move
my body, wasn't expecting this outcome after hearing
many others through the years. I finally stand,
look outside, running shoes in hand, uncertain
if I should go jogging this afternoon where insecure
clouds don't know if they should rain at this hour.
I look up again at deep and silent skies, see doves in flight,

drops of blood on their wings. They trace their way
slowly overhead, weary of escorting black bodies
beyond that hidden place,
burned into the horizon that never forgets.

Last Day of Black History Month

I'm washing pots and pans
early in the morning. Water feels like
hot summer rain of my youth,
playing in rainfall near our red brick house.
Drops shimmering in sunlight,
then magically disappearing.
The water after minutes
of washing dishes: heartless. Scorching.
Don't even notice, don't care.

Teach "Weary Blues" by Langston Hughes
to a restless class, their eyes,
their faces reflecting
how much more of this must we take.
Think about the dripping faucet,
the raindrops in my kitchen sink
while explaining
Jim Crow and Harlem Renaissance
with white, dead chalk in my hand.

White colleagues in hallways
speak with me
about their families,
about the weather,
about their summer plans.
I drop my head, begin making a list:
Tanisha Anderson
George Floyd
Eric Garner
Andre Hill
Manuel Ellis
Stephon Clark
Janisha Fonville—

I stop after someone asks,
What time is it?

Walk outside into rain,
soft, wet, and warm,
falling down
all over our city.

Family Album

Feels like yesterday and the day before.
Each day the same.
Another Black brother dead. Can't keep
up. So many lives, so many names.
Yesterday, it's Earl Moore. 35 years old.
Suffering with hallucinations.
Paramedics yell: "sit up,"
"quit acting stupid," "we ain't
carrying you." Eventually they strap him
face down on the stretcher.
He looks like a flattened car
crushed by a junkyard compactor.

Today, it's Tyre Nichols. 29 years old.
Bad case of driving while Black.
They yank him out. Beat him.
Over and over again. Black and blue bruises.
Blood assaulting the pavement.
Cops yell: "bitch, put your hands
behind your back…," "I'm going to knock
your ass the fuck out." Eventually they lean
his broken body against the squad car.
He looks like twisted, scorched metal
reaching toward a dark
unresponsive sky.

I Know Why the Caged Bird Sings
SAID MAYA ANGELOU

for Elijah McClain

bars were not enough
so we had to do more;
the bars were not enough
so we had to pluck each beautiful feather off
his body; the bars were not enough
so we had to snatch him from behind the bars,
punch him
assault him
rape him of his songs,
but still he kept singing:
"My name is Elijah McClain! I'm different.
I was just going home. I'm just different."
The bars were simply not enough,
so we killed him.
We killed him.

III.

The moon

    follows me

        and

            my grief

On the Evening of My Mother's Death
—July 30, 2018

can't sleep
pacing around the house
I'm now in the kitchen
lost and looking
for something or someone
see a pile of old newspapers,
magazines needing to be thrown away
I look behind me
watch my twin sitting absently at the table

all of us sitting at the kitchen table
eating spaghetti
my favorite
Mom smiles at me
serves another helping but

her chair sits vacant now
and I have to pace again
this time into the living room where
flakes of dust look like snow
on the piano
a picture of Mom and me
smiling on graduation day
I'm wearing a black suit
red tie
she's wearing
a beautiful blue dress
outside on the front porch
sun hugging our backs
next to the picture
there's a pile of Johnson & Johnson bandages
surgical tape
bottles of medicine all

looking out of place
just like the hospital bed
ordered months ago
a temporary arrangement
we thought
I walk over to the front door
look out
across the street
lights off
3:00 a.m.
a dog barks
I keep looking out
waiting for her to come
while I mutter to myself
again and again

Where is she?

she's never coming back
and I will never
be able to sleep again.

I'm the Lost Child Searching for His 84-year-old Father

all rooms look the same
while hunting for 4105, frantic
hide-and-go-seek nightmare,
maneuvering around
winding hospital floor,
sweating, panting inside
this makeshift plastic gown, required
of all visitors, face shield, mask, gloves,
reminds me of my Halloween costume,
an astronaut boy moons ago,
banging on doors, begging for treats,
begging for happiness.

Finally see my father, shivering,
twitching underneath a few white
blankets, the respirator gurgling
in the corner. He opens his eyes,
struggles to say my name,
broken, not the father
I know.

I sit down, stare into his eyes,
try to think of the perfect thing to say,
and my body shakes, but he doesn't notice.
I breathe heavy, rehearse
what to say several times, only *Daddy*
spills out of my mouth as I reach over,
blue latex gloves on, move up and down
his arm, squeeze his hand,
can't feel his skin,
think of what it used to be like—
snug sunlight on swing.

He's carrying me over
his shoulders in the park,
I am taller than the trees,
he spins and spins me around,
I am weightless and the hard
ground lies so far below me.

My Father Is Glass

teetering on the edge
of my kitchen counter
he may fall soon
crash to the floor
I will never be able
to find all of the scattered
pieces once he smashes.
He is breakable
ever since my mother
passed away unexpectedly
we can't talk about it
we are silent with each other
it is like walking on glass
whenever I try to talk with him
about what happened. I'm afraid
of cutting myself
bleeding to death if we do.
He has the military, the battlefields,
the bloodshed,
the dead soldiers he held in his arms
until it earned him the rank
of dead man walking.
Their bodies, their broken
pieces he could never fix.
Maybe he feels this way
about my mother,
regrets that he couldn't
put her back together again.
I stand here in silence
pondering what to say
when I see him again.
I walk away from the kitchen
hear glass shatter
on the cold hard floor
the sound of thunder

singing alto
alone
in the dark.

It Was Four Years Ago

when we thought
you would crawl out
of that hospital bed,
thought you would
walk out those doors,
drive home with us,
roll all the windows down
to feel the calm,
July summer air brush
against your arms and face.
Everything was beautiful that night,
so hopeful, peaceful,
the sound of a few birds
at play, singing a song I didn't know.
The skies were harmless,
not a storm in sight.
Clouds ready for bed
as they began to disappear,
the dark orange sun
calling you to come
home. Then everything changed.
Doctors said nothing
more we can do.
We tried, we tried.
She's gone. I walked
away as they offered explanations.
Four years ago. I still remember
that sick sinking in my stomach.
Knowing things would never be
the same. Things will never be the same.

A Saturday Afternoon Drive

I'm lost while driving down a gravel road
in Gilmer, Texas, where an abandoned gray
metal building stands impolitely
in fields of brown and green grass. It stares
at me, and I start to remember a black
and white photo of my mother, age five,
leaning against a shabby wooden building
ready to crumble with a sneeze. She looks
cut off from the rest of the class, a broken
branch damaged after yesterday's
rain and wind.
I see tall yellow flowers nearby
ready to catch her. My truck stops, I roll
down the window to smell the hot afternoon wind.

Maddening Train

Mom is running around
our wispy house again,
grabbing blouses and shirts,
looks like blue and white streamers
flapping into the wind behind her,
white clouds and blue skies
folding into each other.
She's a maddening train
on a mission, her eyes,
smoke-filled and frantic.
Pulling buttons off
the blouses and shirts,
something new for today.
My father grabs her hands,
tries stopping her.
I beg him: Leave her alone,
let her go, she's not well, she's not
well. Just let her be,
as I drift off to sleep. I wake up,
see a shadowy figure at the foot
of my bed. I am calm, not afraid,
feel comforted in this moment.
I turn on the light. She disappears.

Golden Arches

I.

A billboard featuring
three young white boys, yellow, blue,
red t-shirts, their perfect
teeth, their eternal smiles,
their eyes glowing, holding
hamburgers and cones of ice cream
calls to me while driving down the highway.
I finally see the McDonald's,
want to steal those golden arches,
use them as wings, fly away.

II.

Mother often took me there,
especially when I was a good
boy. I opened my polite mouth,
ordered a Happy Meal.
I beamed like the sun, eating
hamburgers and salty yellow fries,
the salt, tiny snow all over my fingers.
Cartoons characters on the box
always smiling, I never asked why.
Mom kissed my forehead,
I said my prayers, wanted to stay
here in this moment, wanted
everything to last.
She ate the rest of my fries.

III.

I hate seeing those golden arches,
hate remembering bleached

hospital floors, hate remembering
heart monitors, breathing apparatuses,
hate remembering doctors divulging
there is nothing more we can do.
Mother struggles to unwrap the straw
to her drink. I have to help. Her skin is cold.
I'm craving a McDonald's hamburger
loaded with Xanax, want to blot out
those damn arches,
forget my mom's confused plea
they forgot the toy, they forgot the toy
for the very last time.

Sun and Snow

It's strange how a simple
chore—erasing chalk
from the blackboard
after a long hour of writing
words that seemed so permanent—
reminds me of glistening snow
on a winter afternoon
melting away in the sun.

It's strange how
specks of chalk rising
and falling into darkness—
bring back a moment
so profound: sun slanting
through the window
of my mother's hospital
room, dust motes dancing,
my mother
surrounded in snow,
from dust to dust
you will return.

I will be there,
and my father,
and my brothers,
all of us.

In that moment
everything so strange
yet beautiful.
Minutes later
sun and snow
gone.
Everything
gone.

Hearing Her in Longview, TX

My mother's calling.
I close my eyes,
trying hard to imagine
her next to me. She has been
gone too long, so long I miss
calling her, talking with her
about the city life I left behind.
The morning country grass
sings with each step
beneath my feet,
the birds, the cattle,
the goats, the chickens
move about this farmland,
stretching and singing.
The squares along
the wooden fence look
like open windows
during summer, feel
like my mother's
embrace, the warmth,
the color of autumn
sunrise. I hear her
calling my name.
Away from trucks
and cars, hum
of city life, bright night
lights that blind me. Here
I feel alive, unthawed
after working hours
behind a desk.
She calls me
to be silent and still,
to stretch out my arms,
embrace and hold
everything I see

and hear in this moment.
My mother's calling again.
Now she is singing over me.
I lift this warm country
day over my shoulders
before the arrival
of evening moon and stars.

Sleep Tight

she's driving and I'm sitting in the passenger seat
wondering about our destination
tree tops are a perfect green
swaying strangely with this blustery wind
as if listening to a song that does not make sense
we are driving into a tornado
houses are rude hosts on this evening
uprooting themselves and opening doors
to kick out sofas, tables, chairs, china cabinets
I look up again and notice
flying cars in search of where to land
my mother is screaming
yelling at me to help her read the map in my lap
all I see is nothing.

My Mother Ends Her Talking

The thunder's voice finally breaks,
hoarse from all the singing
this afternoon. And the lightning,
tired of flashing sadness and grief,
rushes home for dinner. I sit under
faint light at an empty table, thinking,
wondering how long this stillness
will last. My mother's voice was faint
broken thunder during her final hours,
struggling to talk. Maybe she wanted
to say *I love you* one last time before
the final drops of rain. But her brown
eyes glowed like lightning, trying
to say something from deep within
that she couldn't say.

Goodnight

Dementia robs her of speech today,
words hobble out of her mouth
broken, on crutches, we struggle to make sense of them.
At home, she would point at a book for me
to retrieve off the shelf, one of her
favorites to read in daylight. Placing the book
into her hands, a rainbow came to life.

Now in this cold hospital room,
I look into her hailstormed eyes
and I think I know what she wants
as she points to a bookcase not there.
I recite poetry by Langston Hughes,
Jericho Brown, Maya Angelou
softly into her ear. She smiles, I weep.
She trembles, reaches over to wipe
away a few of my tears.

Stars rush into the room.

Notes

"This Country Does Not Love Us Back" is for Doc Rivers. During a press conference on August 26, 2o2o, Doc Rivers, coach of the LA Clippers, responded to Donald Trump and the Republican National Convention, as well as the Jacob Blake shooting in Kenosha, Wisconsin. He said, "All you hear is Donald Trump and all of them talking about fear. We're the ones getting killed. We're the ones getting shot…We're denied to live in certain communities. We've been hung. We've been shot. And all you do is keep hearing about fear. It's amazing to me why we keep loving this country and this country does not love us back."

"Pumping Gas on a Sunny Day, US Highway 80 in Abilene, TX" is a response to the white supremacist rally on August 11-12, 2017, in Charlottesville, Virginia. Marchers included the alt-right, neo-Confederates, neo-fascists, white nationalists, neo-Nazis, Klansmen, and far-right militias.

"Skittles" is for Treyvon Martin, a 17-year-old African American fatally shot on February 26, 2012, in Sanford, Florida, by George Zimmerman, a member of the neighborhood watch program. President Barack Obama stated: "If I had a son, he'd look like Trayvon… All of us as Americans are going to take this with the seriousness it deserves. Obviously, this is a tragedy. I can only imagine what these parents are going through." After the incident, I walked into my class and stated that Treyvon was me and my twin brother at 17.

"Bulletproof Castles" is for George Floyd, murdered on May 25, 2020, in Minneapolis by Derek Chauvin, a 44-year-old white police officer. George Floyd was 46. The world was in Covid lockdown at the time. I remember all of us being horrified when we watched him die on TV and mobile devices. It made everyone stop in their tracks. In his final minutes, George called out for his mother. He shouted: "Mama… Mama… I'm through!"

"It Feels Like Blood" is for Jayland Walker. Officers fired 94 shots in approximately 6.7 seconds. He died on June 27, 2022. The police pulled him over for an alleged traffic violation. He was 25.

"Another Unarmed Black Man, Earl Moore, 35, Dies in Police Custody." Because our last names are the same, my family wondered if we were related. Related or not, he is another brother who died on December 18, 2022, after being forcefully strapped face down on a stretcher by paramedics in Springfield, Illinois.

"Black Monday" is for Atatiana Jefferson. She was fatally shot inside her home by a Fort Worth, Texas, police officer on October 12, 2019. A neighbor called a non-emergency number after noticing that her front door was open. The name Atatiana reminds me of Saint Tatiana, a Christian martyr in 3rd-century Rome who was a deaconess of the early church.

"Stale Summer Wind" lists some of the unarmed Black people murdered by the police or white citizens: Breonna Taylor, Ahmaud Arbery, Botham Jean, Tamir Rice, Earl Moore, Tyre Nichols, Daunte Wright, and Atatiana Jefferson. The poem also notes Ralph Yarl, a 16-year-old honors student shot twice while going to the wrong house to pick up his twin brothers.

"Jogging with Ahmaud Arbery" is a poem I wrote for Ahmaud Arbery, murdered on February 23, 2020, while jogging in Satilla Shores, Georgia. Three white men were convicted for chasing and killing him. My twin brother and I are runners, and we stopped running for months because of this incident.

"Ahmaud Arbery: Trial Verdict Just Announced" contains the title of this poetry collection. *The Horizon Never Forgets* encourages us to daily remember those Black slaves who lived and died and to also remember black bodies who were murdered and black bodies who still suffer racism today.

"Family Album" is for Tyre Nichols, a 29-year-old Black man fatally injured by police officers in Memphis, Tennessee. He died three days later.

"I Know Why the Caged Bird Sings" is for Elijah McClain, a 23-year-old Black man twice placed in a choke hold and illegally injected with ketamine by paramedics. He went into cardiac arrest because of this incident and was declared brain dead after three days in the hospital. He died on August 24, 2019. The title of this poem is from Maya Angelo's 1969 autobiography. Elijah enjoyed playing the violin and listening to music. During the summer of his death, violinists all over the country played vigils in tribute to him.

Acknowledgments

Grateful thanks to the editors of the following publications where earlier versions of this work first appeared.

The Cry of Black Rage in African American Literature from Frederick Douglass to Richard Wright (scholarly monograph): "Who Am I?"

The Cry of Black Rage in African American Literature from Frederick Douglass to Ta-Nehisi Coates (scholarly monograph): "Pumping Gas on a Sunny Day, US Highway 80 E in Abilene, TX," "Skittles," "Still a Slave," "Stuttering," "Who Am I?"

Spirit of Abilene: An Online Faith Forum: "Amaud Arbery: Trial Verdict Just Announced," "Bulletproof Castles," "Jogging with Ahmaud Arbery"

Thank you to my amazing family for always believing in me.

I would like to express my gratitude to my incredible writing group: Albert Haley, Sherry Rankin, Shelly Sanders, and Debbie Williams. I want to thank Al for allowing me to audit his poetry workshop class years ago. I undoubtedly found my poetic voice because of you. I also extend my appreciation to Shelly for encouraging me to participate in the Texas Association of Creative Writing Teachers in 2023. Things changed for me after that conference.

Special thanks to karla k. morton, the 2010 Texas State Poet Laureate, for profoundly inspiring me to share my poetry with the world. I also would like to thank my dear friends and encouragers of my craft throughout the years: Gregory Straughn, Daniel Ooi, Austin Parsons, Timothy Palmer, Carol Evans, Todd Mountjoy, Thomas Golden, Sandy Freeman, Karen Rich, Micah Heatwole, Gabriel Pedro Prado, Bryan Barnacle, Joshua Gorenflo, Alisha Janette Taylor, Jerry Andrew Taylor, Douglas A. Foster, Ryan Bowman, James Churchill, Randy Harris, Joanna Pambianco, Emily Rankin, Matthew Maxwell, Stanley Wilson, Marianne Wilson, Diana Higgins, Stephanie Hamm, and Ornita and Dwain Burton.

Finally, I am indebted to Kimberly Davis and Linda Parsons at Madville Publishing for believing in both me and this poetry collection.

About the Author

Steven Moore often says that his mother is the wellspring of his poetry. She read and recited poetry to him before his birth and through his growing-up years in locales as varied as Central America and Gurnee, Illinois. Moore received his B.A. in English from the University of Wisconsin-Parkside, and his M.A. and Ph.D. are from the University of Nebraska. The recipient of several teaching and scholarly awards, he is a university professor of English who often teaches poetry workshops and a class called Bon Appétit: Savoring Poetry & Good Cooking. While writing poetry, he immerses himself in jazz, the blues, and the spirit of Langston Hughes. Published widely in literary journals, he is also a bestselling children's author and the author of two scholarly books examining Black rage.

www.ingramcontent.com/pod-product-compliance
Lightning Source LLC
Chambersburg PA
CBHW021418090426
42742CB00009B/1180